Reasons Not to Be Lutheran:
A Complete, Exhaustive and Certain Guide

The singular, authorized edition.
Magisterially researched by
Dr. Thomas D. McAdam

All rights exclusively reserved, April 1, 2016,
Dr. McAdam's Awesomecorp, Ltd.

For the outrage, the giggles, and, of course, the money.

All the Reasons Resourced Exclusively in One Place for Your
Perusal and Meditatio

[Wherein the Lawyers Require we Put Words of Some Kind]
[Where Upon You Mightest Doodle or Take Notes as Thou Wishest]

[Wherein the Lawyers Require we Put Words of Some Kind]
[Where Upon You Mightest Doodle or Take Notes as Thou Wishest]

[Wherein the Lawyers Require we Put Words of Some Kind]
[Where Upon You Mightest Doodle or Take Notes as Thou Wishest]

[Wherein the Lawyers Require we Put Words of Some Kind]
[Where Upon You Mightest Doodle or Take Notes as Thou Wishest]

[Wherein the Lawyers Require we Put Words of Some Kind]
[Where Upon You Mightest Doodle or Take Notes as Thou Wishest]

[Wherein the Lawyers Require we Put Words of Some Kind]
[Where Upon You Mightest Doodle or Take Notes as Thou Wishest]

[Wherein the Lawyers Require we Put Words of Some Kind]
[Where Upon You Mightest Doodle or Take Notes as Thou Wishest]

[Wherein the Lawyers Require we Put Words of Some Kind]
[Where Upon You Mightest Doodle or Take Notes as Thou Wishest]

[Wherein the Lawyers Require we Put Words of Some Kind]
[Where Upon You Mightest Doodle or Take Notes as Thou Wishest]

[Wherein the Lawyers Require we Put Words of Some Kind]
[Where Upon You Mightest Doodle or Take Notes as Thou Wishest]

[Wherein the Lawyers Require we Put Words of Some Kind]
[Where Upon You Mightest Doodle or Take Notes as Thou Wishest]

[Wherein the Lawyers Require we Put Words of Some Kind]
[Where Upon You Mightest Doodle or Take Notes as Thou Wishest]

[Wherein the Lawyers Require we Put Words of Some Kind]
[Where Upon You Mightest Doodle or Take Notes as Thou Wishest]

[Wherein the Lawyers Require we Put Words of Some Kind]
[Where Upon You Mightest Doodle or Take Notes as Thou Wishest]

[Wherein the Lawyers Require we Put Words of Some Kind]
[Where Upon You Mightest Doodle or Take Notes as Thou Wishest]

[Wherein the Lawyers Require we Put Words of Some Kind]
[Where Upon You Mightest Doodle or Take Notes as Thou Wishest]

[Wherein the Lawyers Require we Put Words of Some Kind]
[Where Upon You Mightest Doodle or Take Notes as Thou Wishest]

[Wherein the Lawyers Require we Put Words of Some Kind]
[Where Upon You Mightest Doodle or Take Notes as Thou Wishest]

[Wherein the Lawyers Require we Put Words of Some Kind]
[Where Upon You Mightest Doodle or Take Notes as Thou Wishest]

[Wherein the Lawyers Require we Put Words of Some Kind]
[Where Upon You Mightest Doodle or Take Notes as Thou Wishest]

[Wherein the Lawyers Require we Put Words of Some Kind]
[Where Upon You Mightest Doodle or Take Notes as Thou Wishest]

[Wherein the Lawyers Require we Put Words of Some Kind]
[Where Upon You Mightest Doodle or Take Notes as Thou Wishest]

[Wherein the Lawyers Require we Put Words of Some Kind]
[Where Upon You Mightest Doodle or Take Notes as Thou Wishest]

[Wherein the Lawyers Require we Put Words of Some Kind]
[Where Upon You Mightest Doodle or Take Notes as Thou Wishest]

[Wherein the Lawyers Require we Put Words of Some Kind]
[Where Upon You Mightest Doodle or Take Notes as Thou Wishest]

[Wherein the Lawyers Require we Put Words of Some Kind]
[Where Upon You Mightest Doodle or Take Notes as Thou Wishest]

[Wherein the Lawyers Require we Put Words of Some Kind]
[Where Upon You Mightest Doodle or Take Notes as Thou Wishest]

[Wherein the Lawyers Require we Put Words of Some Kind]
[Where Upon You Mightest Doodle or Take Notes as Thou Wishest]

[Wherein the Lawyers Require we Put Words of Some Kind]
[Where Upon You Mightest Doodle or Take Notes as Thou Wishest]

[Wherein the Lawyers Require we Put Words of Some Kind]
[Where Upon You Mightest Doodle or Take Notes as Thou Wishest]

[Wherein the Lawyers Require we Put Words of Some Kind]
[Where Upon You Mightest Doodle or Take Notes as Thou Wishest]

[Wherein the Lawyers Require we Put Words of Some Kind]
[Where Upon You Mightest Doodle or Take Notes as Thou Wishest]

[Wherein the Lawyers Require we Put Words of Some Kind]
[Where Upon You Mightest Doodle or Take Notes as Thou Wishest]

[Wherein the Lawyers Require we Put Words of Some Kind]
[Where Upon You Mightest Doodle or Take Notes as Thou Wishest]

[Wherein the Lawyers Require we Put Words of Some Kind]
[Where Upon You Mightest Doodle or Take Notes as Thou Wishest]

[Wherein the Lawyers Require we Put Words of Some Kind]
[Where Upon You Mightest Doodle or Take Notes as Thou Wishest]

[Wherein the Lawyers Require we Put Words of Some Kind]
[Where Upon You Mightest Doodle or Take Notes as Thou Wishest]

[Wherein the Lawyers Require we Put Words of Some Kind]
[Where Upon You Mightest Doodle or Take Notes as Thou Wishest]

[Wherein the Lawyers Require we Put Words of Some Kind]
[Where Upon You Mightest Doodle or Take Notes as Thou Wishest]

[Wherein the Lawyers Require we Put Words of Some Kind]
[Where Upon You Mightest Doodle or Take Notes as Thou Wishest]

[Wherein the Lawyers Require we Put Words of Some Kind]
[Where Upon You Mightest Doodle or Take Notes as Thou Wishest]

[Wherein the Lawyers Require we Put Words of Some Kind]
[Where Upon You Mightest Doodle or Take Notes as Thou Wishest]

[Wherein the Lawyers Require we Put Words of Some Kind]
[Where Upon You Mightest Doodle or Take Notes as Thou Wishest]

[Wherein the Lawyers Require we Put Words of Some Kind]
[Where Upon You Mightest Doodle or Take Notes as Thou Wishest]

[Wherein the Lawyers Require we Put Words of Some Kind]
[Where Upon You Mightest Doodle or Take Notes as Thou Wishest]

[Wherein the Lawyers Require we Put Words of Some Kind]
[Where Upon You Mightest Doodle or Take Notes as Thou Wishest]

[Wherein the Lawyers Require we Put Words of Some Kind]
[Where Upon You Mightest Doodle or Take Notes as Thou Wishest]

[Wherein the Lawyers Require we Put Words of Some Kind]
[Where Upon You Mightest Doodle or Take Notes as Thou Wishest]

[Wherein the Lawyers Require we Put Words of Some Kind]
[Where Upon You Mightest Doodle or Take Notes as Thou Wishest]

[Wherein the Lawyers Require we Put Words of Some Kind]
[Where Upon You Mightest Doodle or Take Notes as Thou Wishest]

[Wherein the Lawyers Require we Put Words of Some Kind]
[Where Upon You Mightest Doodle or Take Notes as Thou Wishest]

[Wherein the Lawyers Require we Put Words of Some Kind]
[Where Upon You Mightest Doodle or Take Notes as Thou Wishest]

[Wherein the Lawyers Require we Put Words of Some Kind]
[Where Upon You Mightest Doodle or Take Notes as Thou Wishest]

[Wherein the Lawyers Require we Put Words of Some Kind]
[Where Upon You Mightest Doodle or Take Notes as Thou Wishest]

[Wherein the Lawyers Require we Put Words of Some Kind]
[Where Upon You Mightest Doodle or Take Notes as Thou Wishest]

[Wherein the Lawyers Require we Put Words of Some Kind]
[Where Upon You Mightest Doodle or Take Notes as Thou Wishest]

[Wherein the Lawyers Require we Put Words of Some Kind]
[Where Upon You Mightest Doodle or Take Notes as Thou Wishest]

[Wherein the Lawyers Require we Put Words of Some Kind]
[Where Upon You Mightest Doodle or Take Notes as Thou Wishest]

[Wherein the Lawyers Require we Put Words of Some Kind]
[Where Upon You Mightest Doodle or Take Notes as Thou Wishest]

[Wherein the Lawyers Require we Put Words of Some Kind]
[Where Upon You Mightest Doodle or Take Notes as Thou Wishest]

[Wherein the Lawyers Require we Put Words of Some Kind]
[Where Upon You Mightest Doodle or Take Notes as Thou Wishest]

[Wherein the Lawyers Require we Put Words of Some Kind]
[Where Upon You Mightest Doodle or Take Notes as Thou Wishest]

[Wherein the Lawyers Require we Put Words of Some Kind]
[Where Upon You Mightest Doodle or Take Notes as Thou Wishest]

[Wherein the Lawyers Require we Put Words of Some Kind]
[Where Upon You Mightest Doodle or Take Notes as Thou Wishest]

[Wherein the Lawyers Require we Put Words of Some Kind]
[Where Upon You Mightest Doodle or Take Notes as Thou Wishest]

[Wherein the Lawyers Require we Put Words of Some Kind]
[Where Upon You Mightest Doodle or Take Notes as Thou Wishest]

[Wherein the Lawyers Require we Put Words of Some Kind]
[Where Upon You Mightest Doodle or Take Notes as Thou Wishest]

[Wherein the Lawyers Require we Put Words of Some Kind]
[Where Upon You Mightest Doodle or Take Notes as Thou Wishest]

[Wherein the Lawyers Require we Put Words of Some Kind]
[Where Upon You Mightest Doodle or Take Notes as Thou Wishest]

[Wherein the Lawyers Require we Put Words of Some Kind]
[Where Upon You Mightest Doodle or Take Notes as Thou Wishest]

[Wherein the Lawyers Require we Put Words of Some Kind]
[Where Upon You Mightest Doodle or Take Notes as Thou Wishest]

[Wherein the Lawyers Require we Put Words of Some Kind]
[Where Upon You Mightest Doodle or Take Notes as Thou Wishest]

[Wherein the Lawyers Require we Put Words of Some Kind]
[Where Upon You Mightest Doodle or Take Notes as Thou Wishest]

[Wherein the Lawyers Require we Put Words of Some Kind]
[Where Upon You Mightest Doodle or Take Notes as Thou Wishest]

[Wherein the Lawyers Require we Put Words of Some Kind]
[Where Upon You Mightest Doodle or Take Notes as Thou Wishest]

[Wherein the Lawyers Require we Put Words of Some Kind]
[Where Upon You Mightest Doodle or Take Notes as Thou Wishest]

[Wherein the Lawyers Require we Put Words of Some Kind]
[Where Upon You Mightest Doodle or Take Notes as Thou Wishest]

[Wherein the Lawyers Require we Put Words of Some Kind]
[Where Upon You Mightest Doodle or Take Notes as Thou Wishest]

[Wherein the Lawyers Require we Put Words of Some Kind]
[Where Upon You Mightest Doodle or Take Notes as Thou Wishest]

[Wherein the Lawyers Require we Put Words of Some Kind]
[Where Upon You Mightest Doodle or Take Notes as Thou Wishest]

[Wherein the Lawyers Require we Put Words of Some Kind]
[Where Upon You Mightest Doodle or Take Notes as Thou Wishest]

[Wherein the Lawyers Require we Put Words of Some Kind]
[Where Upon You Mightest Doodle or Take Notes as Thou Wishest]

[Wherein the Lawyers Require we Put Words of Some Kind]
[Where Upon You Mightest Doodle or Take Notes as Thou Wishest]

[Wherein the Lawyers Require we Put Words of Some Kind]
[Where Upon You Mightest Doodle or Take Notes as Thou Wishest]

[Wherein the Lawyers Require we Put Words of Some Kind]
[Where Upon You Mightest Doodle or Take Notes as Thou Wishest]

[Wherein the Lawyers Require we Put Words of Some Kind]
[Where Upon You Mightest Doodle or Take Notes as Thou Wishest]

[Wherein the Lawyers Require we Put Words of Some Kind]
[Where Upon You Mightest Doodle or Take Notes as Thou Wishest]

[Wherein the Lawyers Require we Put Words of Some Kind]
[Where Upon You Mightest Doodle or Take Notes as Thou Wishest]

[Wherein the Lawyers Require we Put Words of Some Kind]
[Where Upon You Mightest Doodle or Take Notes as Thou Wishest]

[Wherein the Lawyers Require we Put Words of Some Kind]
[Where Upon You Mightest Doodle or Take Notes as Thou Wishest]

[Wherein the Lawyers Require we Put Words of Some Kind]
[Where Upon You Mightest Doodle or Take Notes as Thou Wishest]

[Wherein the Lawyers Require we Put Words of Some Kind]
[Where Upon You Mightest Doodle or Take Notes as Thou Wishest]

[Wherein the Lawyers Require we Put Words of Some Kind]
[Where Upon You Mightest Doodle or Take Notes as Thou Wishest]

[Wherein the Lawyers Require we Put Words of Some Kind]
[Where Upon You Mightest Doodle or Take Notes as Thou Wishest]

[Wherein the Lawyers Require we Put Words of Some Kind]
[Where Upon You Mightest Doodle or Take Notes as Thou Wishest]

[Wherein the Lawyers Require we Put Words of Some Kind]
[Where Upon You Mightest Doodle or Take Notes as Thou Wishest]

[Wherein the Lawyers Require we Put Words of Some Kind]
[Where Upon You Mightest Doodle or Take Notes as Thou Wishest]

[Wherein the Lawyers Require we Put Words of Some Kind]
[Where Upon You Mightest Doodle or Take Notes as Thou Wishest]

[Wherein the Lawyers Require we Put Words of Some Kind]
[Where Upon You Mightest Doodle or Take Notes as Thou Wishest]

[Wherein the Lawyers Require we Put Words of Some Kind]
[Where Upon You Mightest Doodle or Take Notes as Thou Wishest]

[Wherein the Lawyers Require we Put Words of Some Kind]
[Where Upon You Mightest Doodle or Take Notes as Thou Wishest]

[Wherein the Lawyers Require we Put Words of Some Kind]
[Where Upon You Mightest Doodle or Take Notes as Thou Wishest]

[Wherein the Lawyers Require we Put Words of Some Kind]
[Where Upon You Mightest Doodle or Take Notes as Thou Wishest]

[Wherein the Lawyers Require we Put Words of Some Kind]
[Where Upon You Mightest Doodle or Take Notes as Thou Wishest]

[Wherein the Lawyers Require we Put Words of Some Kind]
[Where Upon You Mightest Doodle or Take Notes as Thou Wishest]

[Wherein the Lawyers Require we Put Words of Some Kind]
[Where Upon You Mightest Doodle or Take Notes as Thou Wishest]

[Wherein the Lawyers Require we Put Words of Some Kind]
[Where Upon You Mightest Doodle or Take Notes as Thou Wishest]

[Wherein the Lawyers Require we Put Words of Some Kind]
[Where Upon You Mightest Doodle or Take Notes as Thou Wishest]

[Wherein the Lawyers Require we Put Words of Some Kind]
[Where Upon You Mightest Doodle or Take Notes as Thou Wishest]

[Wherein the Lawyers Require we Put Words of Some Kind]
[Where Upon You Mightest Doodle or Take Notes as Thou Wishest]

[Wherein the Lawyers Require we Put Words of Some Kind]
[Where Upon You Mightest Doodle or Take Notes as Thou Wishest]

[Wherein the Lawyers Require we Put Words of Some Kind]
[Where Upon You Mightest Doodle or Take Notes as Thou Wishest]

[Wherein the Lawyers Require we Put Words of Some Kind]
[Where Upon You Mightest Doodle or Take Notes as Thou Wishest]

[Wherein the Lawyers Require we Put Words of Some Kind]
[Where Upon You Mightest Doodle or Take Notes as Thou Wishest]

[Wherein the Lawyers Require we Put Words of Some Kind]
[Where Upon You Mightest Doodle or Take Notes as Thou Wishest]

[Wherein the Lawyers Require we Put Words of Some Kind]
[Where Upon You Mightest Doodle or Take Notes as Thou Wishest]

[Wherein the Lawyers Require we Put Words of Some Kind]
[Where Upon You Mightest Doodle or Take Notes as Thou Wishest]

[Wherein the Lawyers Require we Put Words of Some Kind]
[Where Upon You Mightest Doodle or Take Notes as Thou Wishest]

[Wherein the Lawyers Require we Put Words of Some Kind]
[Where Upon You Mightest Doodle or Take Notes as Thou Wishest]

[Wherein the Lawyers Require we Put Words of Some Kind]
[Where Upon You Mightest Doodle or Take Notes as Thou Wishest]

[Wherein the Lawyers Require we Put Words of Some Kind]
[Where Upon You Mightest Doodle or Take Notes as Thou Wishest]

[Wherein the Lawyers Require we Put Words of Some Kind]
[Where Upon You Mightest Doodle or Take Notes as Thou Wishest]

[Wherein the Lawyers Require we Put Words of Some Kind]
[Where Upon You Mightest Doodle or Take Notes as Thou Wishest]

[Wherein the Lawyers Require we Put Words of Some Kind]
[Where Upon You Mightest Doodle or Take Notes as Thou Wishest]

[Wherein the Lawyers Require we Put Words of Some Kind]
[Where Upon You Mightest Doodle or Take Notes as Thou Wishest]

[Wherein the Lawyers Require we Put Words of Some Kind]
[Where Upon You Mightest Doodle or Take Notes as Thou Wishest]

[Wherein the Lawyers Require we Put Words of Some Kind]
[Where Upon You Mightest Doodle or Take Notes as Thou Wishest]

[Wherein the Lawyers Require we Put Words of Some Kind]
[Where Upon You Mightest Doodle or Take Notes as Thou Wishest]

[Wherein the Lawyers Require we Put Words of Some Kind]
[Where Upon You Mightest Doodle or Take Notes as Thou Wishest]

[Wherein the Lawyers Require we Put Words of Some Kind]
[Where Upon You Mightest Doodle or Take Notes as Thou Wishest]

[Wherein the Lawyers Require we Put Words of Some Kind]
[Where Upon You Mightest Doodle or Take Notes as Thou Wishest]

[Wherein the Lawyers Require we Put Words of Some Kind]
[Where Upon You Mightest Doodle or Take Notes as Thou Wishest]

[Wherein the Lawyers Require we Put Words of Some Kind]
[Where Upon You Mightest Doodle or Take Notes as Thou Wishest]

[Wherein the Lawyers Require we Put Words of Some Kind]
[Where Upon You Mightest Doodle or Take Notes as Thou Wishest]

[Wherein the Lawyers Require we Put Words of Some Kind]
[Where Upon You Mightest Doodle or Take Notes as Thou Wishest]

[Wherein the Lawyers Require we Put Words of Some Kind]
[Where Upon You Mightest Doodle or Take Notes as Thou Wishest]

[Wherein the Lawyers Require we Put Words of Some Kind]
[Where Upon You Mightest Doodle or Take Notes as Thou Wishest]

[Wherein the Lawyers Require we Put Words of Some Kind]
[Where Upon You Mightest Doodle or Take Notes as Thou Wishest]

[Wherein the Lawyers Require we Put Words of Some Kind]
[Where Upon You Mightest Doodle or Take Notes as Thou Wishest]

[Wherein the Lawyers Require we Put Words of Some Kind]
[Where Upon You Mightest Doodle or Take Notes as Thou Wishest]

[Wherein the Lawyers Require we Put Words of Some Kind]
[Where Upon You Mightest Doodle or Take Notes as Thou Wishest]

[Wherein the Lawyers Require we Put Words of Some Kind]
[Where Upon You Mightest Doodle or Take Notes as Thou Wishest]

[Wherein the Lawyers Require we Put Words of Some Kind]
[Where Upon You Mightest Doodle or Take Notes as Thou Wishest]

[Wherein the Lawyers Require we Put Words of Some Kind]
[Where Upon You Mightest Doodle or Take Notes as Thou Wishest]

[Wherein the Lawyers Require we Put Words of Some Kind]
[Where Upon You Mightest Doodle or Take Notes as Thou Wishest]

[Wherein the Lawyers Require we Put Words of Some Kind]
[Where Upon You Mightest Doodle or Take Notes as Thou Wishest]

[Wherein the Lawyers Require we Put Words of Some Kind]
[Where Upon You Mightest Doodle or Take Notes as Thou Wishest]

[Wherein the Lawyers Require we Put Words of Some Kind]
[Where Upon You Mightest Doodle or Take Notes as Thou Wishest]

[Wherein the Lawyers Require we Put Words of Some Kind]
[Where Upon You Mightest Doodle or Take Notes as Thou Wishest]

[Wherein the Lawyers Require we Put Words of Some Kind]
[Where Upon You Mightest Doodle or Take Notes as Thou Wishest]

[Wherein the Lawyers Require we Put Words of Some Kind]
[Where Upon You Mightest Doodle or Take Notes as Thou Wishest]

[Wherein the Lawyers Require we Put Words of Some Kind]
[Where Upon You Mightest Doodle or Take Notes as Thou Wishest]

[Wherein the Lawyers Require we Put Words of Some Kind]
[Where Upon You Mightest Doodle or Take Notes as Thou Wishest]

[Wherein the Lawyers Require we Put Words of Some Kind]
[Where Upon You Mightest Doodle or Take Notes as Thou Wishest]

[Wherein the Lawyers Require we Put Words of Some Kind]
[Where Upon You Mightest Doodle or Take Notes as Thou Wishest]

[Wherein the Lawyers Require we Put Words of Some Kind]
[Where Upon You Mightest Doodle or Take Notes as Thou Wishest]

[Wherein the Lawyers Require we Put Words of Some Kind]
[Where Upon You Mightest Doodle or Take Notes as Thou Wishest]

[Wherein the Lawyers Require we Put Words of Some Kind]
[Where Upon You Mightest Doodle or Take Notes as Thou Wishest]

[Wherein the Lawyers Require we Put Words of Some Kind]
[Where Upon You Mightest Doodle or Take Notes as Thou Wishest]

[Wherein the Lawyers Require we Put Words of Some Kind]
[Where Upon You Mightest Doodle or Take Notes as Thou Wishest]

[Wherein the Lawyers Require we Put Words of Some Kind]
[Where Upon You Mightest Doodle or Take Notes as Thou Wishest]

[Wherein the Lawyers Require we Put Words of Some Kind]
[Where Upon You Mightest Doodle or Take Notes as Thou Wishest]

[Wherein the Lawyers Require we Put Words of Some Kind]
[Where Upon You Mightest Doodle or Take Notes as Thou Wishest]

[Wherein the Lawyers Require we Put Words of Some Kind]
[Where Upon You Mightest Doodle or Take Notes as Thou Wishest]

[Wherein the Lawyers Require we Put Words of Some Kind]
[Where Upon You Mightest Doodle or Take Notes as Thou Wishest]

[Wherein the Lawyers Require we Put Words of Some Kind]
[Where Upon You Mightest Doodle or Take Notes as Thou Wishest]

[Wherein the Lawyers Require we Put Words of Some Kind]
[Where Upon You Mightest Doodle or Take Notes as Thou Wishest]

[Wherein the Lawyers Require we Put Words of Some Kind]
[Where Upon You Mightest Doodle or Take Notes as Thou Wishest]

[Wherein the Lawyers Require we Put Words of Some Kind]
[Where Upon You Mightest Doodle or Take Notes as Thou Wishest]

[Wherein the Lawyers Require we Put Words of Some Kind]
[Where Upon You Mightest Doodle or Take Notes as Thou Wishest]

[Wherein the Lawyers Require we Put Words of Some Kind]
[Where Upon You Mightest Doodle or Take Notes as Thou Wishest]

[Wherein the Lawyers Require we Put Words of Some Kind]
[Where Upon You Mightest Doodle or Take Notes as Thou Wishest]

[Wherein the Lawyers Require we Put Words of Some Kind]
[Where Upon You Mightest Doodle or Take Notes as Thou Wishest]

[Wherein the Lawyers Require we Put Words of Some Kind]
[Where Upon You Mightest Doodle or Take Notes as Thou Wishest]

[Wherein the Lawyers Require we Put Words of Some Kind]
[Where Upon You Mightest Doodle or Take Notes as Thou Wishest]

[Wherein the Lawyers Require we Put Words of Some Kind]
[Where Upon You Mightest Doodle or Take Notes as Thou Wishest]

[Wherein the Lawyers Require we Put Words of Some Kind]
[Where Upon You Mightest Doodle or Take Notes as Thou Wishest]

[Wherein the Lawyers Require we Put Words of Some Kind]
[Where Upon You Mightest Doodle or Take Notes as Thou Wishest]

[Wherein the Lawyers Require we Put Words of Some Kind]
[Where Upon You Mightest Doodle or Take Notes as Thou Wishest]

[Wherein the Lawyers Require we Put Words of Some Kind]
[Where Upon You Mightest Doodle or Take Notes as Thou Wishest]

[Wherein the Lawyers Require we Put Words of Some Kind]
[Where Upon You Mightest Doodle or Take Notes as Thou Wishest]

[Wherein the Lawyers Require we Put Words of Some Kind]
[Where Upon You Mightest Doodle or Take Notes as Thou Wishest]

[Wherein the Lawyers Require we Put Words of Some Kind]
[Where Upon You Mightest Doodle or Take Notes as Thou Wishest]

[Wherein the Lawyers Require we Put Words of Some Kind]
[Where Upon You Mightest Doodle or Take Notes as Thou Wishest]

[Wherein the Lawyers Require we Put Words of Some Kind]
[Where Upon You Mightest Doodle or Take Notes as Thou Wishest]

[Wherein the Lawyers Require we Put Words of Some Kind]
[Where Upon You Mightest Doodle or Take Notes as Thou Wishest]

Thus, resteth the unanswerable case.

Made in the USA
Monee, IL
20 February 2020